The advent of the coeducational International Volleyball Association proved what volleyball players have known for years—that top-flight volleyball is a great women's sport, too. And now that women have taken their place as equals beside men in the professional IVA, Mary Jo Peppler, the only woman player/coach in the IVA, has written a book especially for women who want to know how they can become expert volleyball players.

But she has not written the usual kind of how-to book of skills and fundamentals—though those are all here, to be sure, including movement, serving, passing, volleying, diving, rolling, and defense. Rather, Peppler has written a how-to book that is also a statement of philosophy about participating as a woman in sport, showing that psychology and attitudes are as much a part of volleyball as basic skills and techniques. Every woman athlete will want to know what Peppler has to say in this distinctive book.

inside
volleyball
for women

mary jo peppler

henry regnery company · chicago

Library of Congress Cataloging in Publication Data

Peppler, Mary Jo, 1944-
    Inside volleyball for women.

    Includes index.
    1. Volleyball for women.   I. Title.
GV1017.V6P44   796.32′5   76-55656
ISBN 0-8092-7943-6
ISBN 0-8092-7942-8 pbk.

Published by Henry Regnery Company
180 North Michigan Avenue, Chicago, Illinois 60601
Manufactured in the United States of America
Library of Congress Catalog Card Number: 76-55656
International Standard Book Number: 0-8092-7943-6 (cloth)
                                    0-8092-7942-8 (paper)

Published simultaneously in Canada by
Beaverbooks
953 Dillingham Road
Pickering, Ontario L1W 1Z7
Canada

acknowledgments

Thank you to Canon, USA, in particular Bill Wuest and Jerry Anderson, for their cooperation with photographic equipment.

A special thanks to Carol Dewey for adding her beautiful photographs to this book. This venture gives me a particular joy and satisfaction since it marks the first of what will hopefully be a multitude of grand ideas upon which we have not lost money.

Thanks to the many people who assisted EPU in its impassioned amateur struggle for the chance to become the best in the world.

Thanks to Pat Zartman for his part in my development as a coach. His contributions have always been professional and technologically sound.

And, finally, a thanks to my mother.

dedication

Dedicated to Marilyn McReavy,
with whom I have struggled for volleyball
excellence most of my adult life.
Together we have developed coaching
and playing knowledges, skills,
philosophies, and successes.

contents

Of all the information presented to you in this book, by far the most important thing for you to learn is TO TRY. Unfortunately a strange thing has happened in our country: somehow it has become acceptable to lose if you do not try. In fact it sometimes seems that the ultimate "cool" is to win without trying. This may be an outgrowth of what *appears* to be effortlessness on the part of super-athletes. Actually, any movements that appear effortless are the result of years and years of diligent practice. Do not mistake a long background of hard work for not trying!

As an athlete or a person, do not contribute to a warped sense of what is "cool." Remember that it is never "cool" to *not try*. Much of the appeal of the television *Superstars* contest to the public is seeing some of the best athletes in the world lose their apparent "cool" by trying to perform without having the training and skills to be "cool." Everyone can relate to this experience because a lot of the difference between a professional athlete and a weekend athlete is TRAINING AND SKILLS. The superstar working out of his or her element is working with the same undeveloped tools everyone else has. As a result he does not have the smoothness and efficiency that the years of training have given to him in his special sport. Superstars are "cool" *as a result of being skilled and trained*. Their efforts are more often channeled efficiently than are the amateur's and therefore appear to be effortless. Believe me, nobody reaches the top without trying hard.

In fact, it is always better to try. Even though sometimes subtle pressures seem to indicate that it is degrading to try and fail, remember that it is never degrading to try, nor is it ever degrading to fail if you have tried your best. By not trying, many people think they have shifted the emphasis of the competition and thereby have degraded the situation rather than themselves. Many athletes get into the "not trying" syndrome unconsciously. Be sure you have set your athletic environment so that you always have the freedom to try.

You must learn to accept conditions and play for the best of the team. If you cannot accept the conditions then find another situation. One of the worst kinds of athlete is the constant griper; this person makes himself and everyone around him miserable. Keep your goals in mind at all times. The harder you personally try to be an accomplished athlete and try to make your team successful the better your experience will be and the more you will develop as a person. Remember, it is not EVER acceptable to lose if you did not try; in my opinion not trying is the worst of all possible sins. Rather, I would hope that you too will try hard at everything you wish to accomplish. This is a value you will hopefully incorporate into your lifestyle.

VOLLEYBALL CAN BE a totally demanding physical sport on the highest levels. Those athletes at the top are in fantastic shape!

chapter 1
WINNING

WINNING

Americans are preoccupied with winning. When Olga Korbut went home from the 1976 Olympics with only a silver medal, everyone asked "What happened?" She scored only 9.9 in some of her events whereupon ABC reviewed her performance in stop action and slow motion pointing out exactly where she displayed evidence of being less than perfect.

Yes, Olga was only second in the world. Only. She was one whole tenth of a point from being perfect! But she did not win.

It is amazing to me that although only one team, or one individual can win in any contest, that the multitudes continue to compete. In this country of free choice, one cannot choose to win. One can choose to lose (and many do daily). However, one can only choose to "try" to win. Yet the number of losers compared to the number of winners does not seem to warrant the attempt. Why would you choose to "try to win" when you know the odds are against

your success. Especially since, in our country at least, losers are dogs. As a result, many people have developed such a fear of failure that they never actually "try to win," always holding back enough that an excuse for losing is built in. I think this is the wrong approach. One should have to answer for "not trying to win" rather than for not winning. Nobody can completely control winning—there are too many factors outside of yourself with which to contend. Given certain conditions, you can always "try to win." The only real winners in life are those individuals who are able to throw themselves completely into the effort of accomplishment. This is what makes *trying* full of fun and enthusiasm. If you cannot play volleyball with fun and enthusiasm, if you cannot find satisfaction in "trying your best" to win regardless of the outcome, if you feel no reward in developing personally and expanding your capabilities in every area that sports—and specifically volleyball—offer to you, then please don't participate.

Trying to win is many times more difficult for women than it is for men. Unfortunately, most women are uncomfortable in a competitive environment. Unlike men who are environmentally trained to handle situations in life by confrontation, most women are traditionally taught to handle situations by manipulation. Competition is direct confrontation. Until you welcome the challenge of competition openly, are demanding of yourself, and try for excellence, you will not become a good competitor. Many times I am asked about fear in connection with competition. My opinion is that most fear is a fear of unknowns. There are several types of unknowns to deal with in a match. Here are some of them:

1. It is unknown how you will react or perform.

2. It is unknown how good your opponents will be and in what ways they will be good.

3. It is unknown what form the game will take and what factors will ultimately determine who will win.

4. Oftentimes the environment is unfamiliar and therefore uncomfortable.

5. It is unknown what kind of effect additional persons will have on the match: the official, the crowd, your teammates, etc.

6. It is unknown what all the unknowns are.

It is possible to prepare yourself well enough to eliminate many of the unknowns, but some will always remain. If you learn to welcome these factors as an exciting challenge, you will begin to view competition as fun and begin to look forward to it. Ask yourself why you are involved. It would be silly to practice diligently day after day and then dread competition. The competition is for what you should be practicing. You should welcome the unknowns of a match with excited anticipation. Competition is a challenge to extend your abilities. Winning or losing, you as an individual are developing. Sometimes the most important progress I have made as a player and as an individual has occurred in retrospect of a loss. Winning and losing are usually only relative to your opponent and have nothing to do with perfection, which should be your goal. I've known players who mull over a game many weeks after its completion, reviewing what they should have done. If you try your very best every time you compete, you will be operating with all the skills you possess. Each time you compete, it will be with increased ability, skill, and knowledge. If you did not do something which would have helped you win the game, but you were trying your best, then you were not capable of doing that thing at that time. Highly skilled and experienced players are the result of many hours of practice and have experienced many combinations of failure and success. They can recognize the solution to a multitude of situations because they have seen them before. By welcoming competition you will soon learn these combinations too.

There is no disgrace in losing. Ask yourself after *every* competition if you did your very best. If you can answer "yes!" then you must accept the results regardless of the outcome. However, if you answer "no," whether you have won or lost you have cheated yourself.

YOU AND YOUR FEMININITY

Many women athletes who achieve excellence come to a point in their career when they feel they must make a choice between being feminine and being good at their sport. Making a choice between the two is not the only solution and most women find that they can arrive at an alternate end.

The identity crisis that women face in sports are similar to the problems women in every field experience. Most professions are traditionally male-dominated. Most have certainly been developed by men for men. In fact, sports are nearly synonymous with masculinity and therefore in sports we find the extreme case of the female adapting to the male environment. If sport can make a man out of a boy, what does it do for a woman? As females, if we try to accept unconditionally the total package presented to us from the male sports experience, there most certainly will be identity conflicts.

As an athlete, you will no doubt come to a point in your training when you are going to think twice before you lift weights, sweat, grunt and groan, or beat your boyfriend at tennis. These are not normal "lady-like" activities. Nonetheless, just the fact that you are female should not exclude you from them. Women must shape their own amateur and professional sports so that they are consistent with positive female values. In this way, a woman can become more feminine through her involvement in sports. Women should not have to be concerned with becoming "equal" to men in sports. Women's sports should not mold themselves after male models. The quicker we realize that the female sports product is very much different from the male sports product, the earlier we can integrate sports and the female personality. Positive dynamics of the feminine contribution to sports must be identified and developed.

Women will presently find differences in their approach to sports from men in the areas of motivation, movement, and competitive attitudes.

MOTIVATION

Male sports contain a good deal of competition for supremacy over an opponent. One-up-manship is prevalent especially in "really masculine" sports. I think women should compete to strive for personal goals. Perfection is the ideal. Nothing is proven by being the first to beat any individual opponent. Reaching out toward a perfection which you imagine or is accepted in your sport will give you a healthy view of your participation. Trying to win is inherent in the perfection of any confrontation sport; winning is a welcome by-product. Competition should never be a confrontation of ego supremacy. However, the competition of two wills to be perfect is part of any contest.

MOVEMENT

Women are trained to view movement—especially strong, aggressive movements related to sports—as functional. Men view these same movements as means to gain recognition or to "show-off." Movements which raise one's status within the group or draw attention are of great interest to male athletes. In fact, certain movements usually become culturally impressive within certain sports. Women tend to be more interested in movements which contribute to sound skills.

Men approach power in sport as a means of domination. Women appreciate power more as it relates to performance of skill than to ego supremacy. As a result, I believe that women are easily channeled toward skills, finesse, and strategy.

COMPETITIVE ATTITUDES

Many women are much more adept at manipulating their environment than confronting it. As a result of "absorbing" most of their environment, women become sensitive. This opens great channels to communication and leads to tremendous potential for team sports. Further, it alerts women to the early indications of the vicissitudes of competition, thus giving a capacity for adaptable, changeable competition. From a spectator point of view, this should introduce lots of surprise.

Because women are comfortable operating covertly, we are willing to work and wait for results. If this is directed positively, great results can ensue.

YOUR CHOICE

Women are emerging in sports—today is an exciting time to be involved. Do not sacrifice your femininity because you happen to come head-to-head with some values that would normally "make a man out of you." Having a healthy and comfortable appreciation of your own sexuality will make you a good competitor and a happy person. Athletes who do not have a solid identity will not be able to rely upon themselves when the competition gets really tough. Believing in yourself and accepting yourself are what will make you a confident athlete and woman. When you encounter male-directed values in your sport, review the factors and consider them in light of your femininity. You do not need to reject sports or any of its successes, merely put the apparent conflicts in their proper perspective. Experience your femininity in all realms of life and let your involvement in sports make you feel more feminine, more confident, and more successful than ever before.

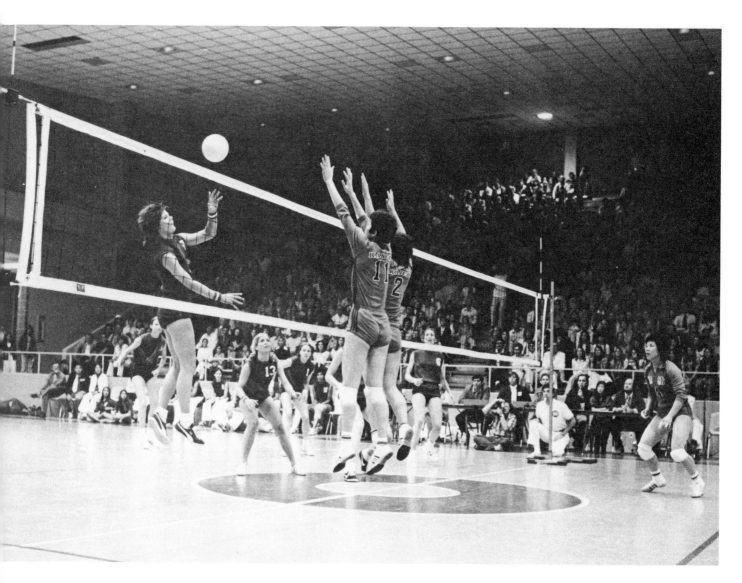

VOLLEYBALL CLOTHING SHOULD compliment the sport.

chapter 2
HOW TO BECOME A VOLLEYBALL PLAYER

Before we get down to brass tacks and start getting technical about volleyball, I think that it is high time we identified the imposters from the real thing. Millions of people all over the United States play volleyball. People play volleyball as representatives of their country, in school, in church, in recreational and industrial leagues, in the parks and in their own back yards. Except for the net and the ball, the sport is barely recognizable.

THE REAL THING

To set the record straight, I would like to discuss how to recognize a "real" volleyball player. Volleyball is a game of efficiency: movements must be efficient and clothing must be efficient if your body is to be efficient. First, you should take pride in your body. Volleyball can be a totally demanding physical sport on the highest levels. Those athletes at the top are in fantastic shape. This means that you must make ev-

ery effort to be slim and trim, with good muscle tone. If you have the choice of being sloppy or neat, by all means be neat! If you want to be a volleyball player, you first must do what you can to get your body prepared for the sport. This might be a pretty big job in the sense that it could include a full-time attitude toward yourself. Whenever possible, on or off the court, you should practice efficiency in everything that you do. You must learn to respect your body and never abuse it. You must learn to have as much control of it in as many situations as possible. I think that drugs and alcohol are degrading for any athlete, but their use is especially disgusting for a volleyball player. First, use of anything artificial upsets the mental, physical, and spiritual agreement you have with your psyche. These artificial catalysts make you dependent upon something external to fulfill needs or create reactions. In an ideal sense, a true athlete should train to have a complete understanding with her total self so that she

STRONG, HEALTHY, AND efficient bodies are part of the beauty of the sport of volleyball.

commitment to perfection in your total life. Just remember that whether or not you are an athlete is your choice; and it is not necessary to become an athlete to enjoy playing volleyball. Many enjoy sports for a myriad of reasons including health, recreation and as a deviation from their usual pursuits. The values of sports are commensurate with their particular focus in an individual's life. Find what place sports play in your life and act accordingly. I think there is some place for sports in everyone's life.

CLOTHES MAKE THE PLAYER?

Because volleyball is a sport of total efficiency at its best, its clothes are also efficient. You should try to become confident of your body by spending the necessary time training it. Strong, healthy and efficient bodies are part of the beauty of the sport of volleyball, and this should be your goal. While playing volleyball your clothing should compliment the sport. Short shorts that are snug around the leg are the best, as well as form-fitting body shirts of any sleeve length that suits you. Volleyball players usually tuck their shirts in; numbering or lettering on the shirts should not be rubberized or sticky in any way because you will be sliding around the floor too much. Rubberized numbers afford unwanted and sometimes shocking halts in your follow-through movements. I would like to go on record as stating that volleyball players do *not* wear knee socks! Knee pads are a usual part of anyone's volleyball equipment, but they may become optional when you become an accomplished player. If you are primarily a diver, you will probably not need them; if you roll more and use your knees to get up you had better use knee pads. However you can learn to roll without touching your knees to the floor and thereby eliminate one more cumbersome bit of clothing. Volleyball players do *not* wear knee pads in order to slide around on their knees. Knee-sliding is a bad habit

can achieve anything that she desires by willing it. There should be no need for drugs. Although this is a difficult goal to strive toward, it is well worth the rewards. Many athletes achieve this type of perfection on the court and for most it becomes a way of life off of the court. If you think that being an athlete is performing a certain way at practices and contests and then going about your life with a totally different set of values the rest of the day, please do not define yourself as an athlete. Realizing that being an athlete is a way of life can help you decide whether or not becoming an athlete is a good choice for you. Many do not realize that becoming an athlete is a full time

HOW WELL YOU play the sport is directly related to how much you put into it. If you want more, give more!

and a sloppy technique. Women volleyball players should always make an effort to look and feel feminine. Remember that by having a healthy and comfortable appreciation of your own sexuality, you will become a better competitor and a happier person.

INDIVIDUAL RESPONSIBILITY

You must assume the individual responsibility for making yourself the type of volleyball player that you want to become. Anything that anyone does for you which helps you become better should be viewed as a bonus. If you want eventually to become a professional, your first step is to make yourself skillful and in top condition to perform. Your mental attitudes and readiness to play are always your job. Many volleyball players play the game for the approval of the coach, status from their peers, or prestige within their community. These players are not pro candidates. In fact, they are not even playing the game to reach their own personal level of perfection and they are not accepting personal responsibility for their own development. These

so called players will never reach anything near excellence because they are not in charge of their own future. One of the best things that participation in sports can offer an individual is the opportunity to learn a reliance upon herself. It has been my experience that many female athletes are not self-reliant. So regardless of what level of play you have chosen for yourself, you must accept full responsibility for getting there and staying there. How well you play is directly related to how much you put into it. Do not be disappointed that you cannot perform some of the more advanced skills if you only practice once a week. You will get what you give to a sport; if you want more —*give more*!

Since the first step toward accomplishment of anything begins with individual responsibility, which is also the first stage of leadership, you must develop total reliance upon yourself for your own accomplishments. This also means taking personal responsibility for failure. You can always be better; you could have always done something different that would have made you or your teammates successful: no excuses

THE ONLY WAY to become successful is to *try*.

please! Don't be afraid of failure either. You should welcome (though not pursue) failure as a learning experience. Many players who are not self-reliant become afraid to try. The only way to become successful is to try. Sometimes the best situations in which to really analyze yourself are those in which you fail miserably. Failure is often associated with stress situations; you can welcome stress when it offers opportunity for accomplishment in any part of your life. Try to free yourself to try anything. A positive and fearless approach to success and failure should become a part of your self concept.

MOTIVATION

If you want to become the best, you have to work hard. It can be hard to train every day, to push yourself physically, to force yourself to concentrate, and to discipline yourself whenever you practice. It is even harder to live with these same principles every minute of your life. Nonetheless you cannot be easy on yourself. If you want to become a superior athlete now, you must constantly nudge yourself toward excellence. Motivation can only come from within. You must not rely upon your teammates or

your parents for it. They cannot make you perform at game point; they cannot make you run that last wind sprint when it is cold and windy on the track and you are all alone and exhausted. Only you can have the desire to force yourself to continue. And only you can really know the complete satisfaction of accomplishment. It is your life. Sure, we all get down some days and are lazy others, but we have to keep our heads on straight and our goals well defined and close at hand. Your first accomplishment must be the direction of yourself. The somebody who must take over when you feel that you cannot go on has got to be you. Every time you walk into the gymnasium, you must take responsibility for motivating yourself. You must always be ready for a concentrated effort at practice. You must always be prepared for your best performance when you walk into the arena for a competition. These are all part of your job if you choose to become an athlete.

If you have decided to fit volleyball into a less significant portion of your life, your emphasis of course will be different. In this case you must practice volleyball with just enough intensity to satisfy the personal goal you have set for yourself. I think that everyone can enjoy sport for the personal

EVERY TIME YOU walk into the gymnasium, you must take the responsibility for motivating yourself. You must always be prepared for your best performance when you walk into the arena for competition.

perfection with which they can be rewarded, even though the goal may be dictated by a number of self-imposed limitations.

YOUR TEAMMATES

When you first start playing, your primary energies will naturally be directed toward making yourself the best player possible under your particular conditions. As you begin to mature as a player you should start accepting some of the responsibility for the performance of the whole team. There is always something that you can do to make your team a little more successful. You should, in fact, take pride in not letting your teammates fail. If your teammate hits the ball into the block, you should extend yourself trying to cover her; if she makes a bad pass, you must do everything possible to make a good set with as little effort as possible. By making your effort look easy, your teammates may not have such a feeling of failure when the ball did not go to exactly the right place. You must transcend petty jealousy and dislike. During a game you must be prepared to strive all out for your teammates. You do not have to mix your personal life with theirs, but when you intermix with them in the atmosphere of

sport you must respect them as you do yourself; their success is imperative to your personal well-being. Through volleyball, your teammates will become an extension of yourself. If you cannot adopt an attitude approaching this concept, you should not be a team sport competitor.

SELF ANALYSIS

Once you make the commitment to become a volleyball player, do not just jump into it blindly. You would not buy the first pair of shoes you saw, and I know that you would shop around before you put money down on a new car. Do not just become any kind of volleyball player either. Shop around! Take a look at what you like to watch in a volleyball player; consider what your body type and talents are and how much time and energy you are willing to dedicate to your development. Finally adopt a style which is distinctly your own. The Japanese women were the best in the world for a long time, and yet they were probably the smallest world-class team in the field. Russia dominated the last decade (until 1974 when Japan regained the crown) by being stronger, bigger, and steadier than all the others. Find out what is your bag and create your style to suit it. Do not be ready

THESE SHORT KOREAN players (number 5 is 5'4") do not let their height handicap them. Pick a style of play that suits your body type.

to give up with ideas such as, "I'm too small," or "I guess I'm just too slow!" With dedicated specific training and a style which utilizes your strengths, you can satisfy your goal of becoming a certain kind of volleyball player. Almost everybody has to be somewhere between the short, disciplined Japanese athletes and the tall, strong Russians. At both ends of the spectrum are world-class styles. With a little work you can find a world-class style of your own to pursue.

PRACTICE

Once you have settled upon a style which you will no doubt alter significantly as time goes on, you must begin to train. You must make yourself as strong, as quick, and as smart as you can. The first step is personal conditioning; the second step is mastering the skills of the game; and the final touch is to learn to be smarter than everyone else in the game. I would recommend becoming down-right sneaky. What you cannot find

out about the game from books and people in the game, you will have to discover for yourself. If you do not have dedicated teammates, become a salesperson. In other words, if you want to reach excellence, nothing can stop you. Whatever level you set for yourself to reach, you must be prepared to reach it through steady, hard work.

If you are really serious about making the big time, beginning with two hours of training each day is not at all unreasonable. You should never practice unless you are making it meaningful. This does not mean to quit when things are not going your way since continuing to practice when you are struggling is often the most rewarding type of practice. Instead, you must make practice meaningful by continuing to try. If you do not try mentally, physically, and emotionally it is not meaningful. If this book does not teach you anything else, I hope it will teach you that *you have to try*! Unless you try, any experience in life is far from being fulfilling.

VOLLEYBALL IS CONTAGIOUS. It has reached epidemic proportions around the world and is also becoming addictive in the United States. There is no other sport like it.

chapter 3
THE NATURE OF THE GAME

What is the big deal about volleyball anyhow? Why is it so popular as both a spectator and participant sport throughout the world? What makes it so different? Why are officials shot in South America? Why was the volleyball final one of the first sports sold out at the 1976 Olympics? Why are youngsters who show aptitude for the sport in Russia channeled into volleyball schools?

Volleyball is contagious. It has reached epidemic proportions around the world and is also becoming addictive in the U. S. There is no other sport like it.

MOVEMENT

Just looking at the movement requirements of the game gives one some idea as to its unusual demands. Most noticeable of the movement peculiarities is that volleyball is a rebound sport. This is particularly different for Americans since most popular American sports are possession sports, such as football and basketball. Volleyball is primarily a movement sport. Preparation for contact is as important as contact. Many times supportive or extension movement is as important as movement which leads to the contact. Even when a player makes contact with the ball it is only an intermediate step or a part of a chain. All volleyball contact is ruled by cause and effect. The ball is never stationary. There are no stalls. A player may never wait for a certain circumstance to develop. The conditions are probably a little bit different each time contact is made. Each contact is so dependent upon the sum of a team's combined effort (supportive as well as contact) that it is nearly impossible for an individual to take over and single-handedly determine or reverse the outcome of a game or match.

Further, forearm contact is unique to volleyball. It is extremely uncomfortable for beginners to try to use their forearms as a contact surface. Another uncomfortable and unnatural aspect of the game for beginners is the game's demand on your body

17

TOTAL MOVEMENT ZONES characterize the sport. Players must be able to
contact the ball from inches off of the floor, to . . .

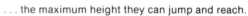

. . . the maximum height they can jump and reach.

to move through total movement zones. The ball can and will be played inches from the floor with your body fully extended horizontally at the same height or vertically to the very maximum height you can jump and reach. No implements or pads are used. Unlike many sports which are familiar to us, volleyball utilizes almost no rotational movement and nearly all movements are in body line.

PECULIARITIES OF THE GAME

The rules afford many unique qualities to the sport. Since volleyball is determined by points instead of time, the game is never lost until the final moment of victory or defeat. This single factor is what I think is one of the greatest spectator attractions of the game. While the game is in progress, it can always be won. I have seen time and time again teams returning from large point deficits to win a game. It is not uncommon in three-out-of-five-game matches for a team to lose the first two games and continue to win the match. Momentum switches frequently and dramatically, making the game constantly exciting and unpredictable. There are rarely long waits between periods when the ball is put into play, so there is not much rest for the players nor is there much rest for the spectators. In fact, cardiac arrest is the most common volleyball spectator injury. The excitement peaks are brutal on an ill-trained circulatory system. I think it is not at all out of order to put your most avid supporters on a training schedule so they can last the entire season without injury.

In the amateur game there is a limitation on substitutions which eliminates specialization. You must rotate; this gives each player six new orientations throughout the match. Different positions, different people playing next to you, demand great versatility on your part.

The rules govern techniques rigidly. Therefore, not only are you penalized for having bad skills by lack of ball control, you are further penalized by the referee who takes the ball away from you.

There is a time-out limitation, therefore you get only limited rest and your coach has only limited contact with you during the match. You must learn to rely upon yourself. The ratio of the size of the court to the amount of people occupying it makes volleyball one of the most congested, and therefore a most severely demanding, team sport. The people, court size, number of hits, and speed of the ball make the number of combinations of things that can happen in a volleyball match awesome. This makes the sport constantly surprising with plenty of room for innovation.

THE COMPETITIVE NATURE OF VOLLEY-BALL

The nature of competition in a volleyball match is also slightly different from most sports. It is easy to avoid one-on-one confrontations. This makes the sport further technique-oriented. It is difficult to be aggressive in the sport. The space limitation and demand for teamwork makes aggressiveness a favorable quality only when roles and zones have been clearly defined. Only when a player has determined her own responsibilities in relationship to the team goals, systems, and mannerisms and capabilities of her teammates, can her aggressiveness actually benefit the team. Discerning the fine line between individual responsibility and extending her ego into the team is a tricky problem. There is very little overt autonomy and lots of subtle autonomy. By contrast, one must often appear to sublimate her ego for the good of the team. The success of one's teammates is critical to the success of the team as is one's own performance. Since contact with the ball is only an intermediate goal, a player is always working to "better the ball," or make each successive contact on the ball better and better. Your effort is merely a partial contribution to the total effort. How much your contact on the ball or effort in a

VOLLEYBALL IS A team sport. The degree of cooperation between teammates is what determines a team's success.

match has to do with the total outcome of the rally or the match is fully dependent upon the nature of your teammates' contributions. In this sense, volleyball is the perfect team game.

Strangely, volleyball *offenses* do not "make points"—they prevent points. Conversely, *defense* wins or scores the points. It is most difficult to develop good carry-over practice drills for the sport. In practice, we work at keeping the ball in play, whereas in competition, the ultimate end is to make the "kill."

There are many more idiosyncracies to the sport of volleyball. As an aspiring player, you should become sensitive to these differences so you can best cope with the environment in which you are placing yourself. The most important thing to learn about the sport, of course, is to love it.

A SOLID SKILL will not let you down in stress situations.

chapter 4
LEARNING THE SKILLS

Learning skills is the first step an athlete must take before she can participate in any sport with any amount of efficiency. No matter how good your coach is, the ultimate responsibility for skills will eventually come to rest on your shoulders. A coach cannot "give" you skills—you can master skills personally only through hours and hours of practice. How good you become is therefore determined by how much time and effort you are willing to devote to excellence.

Before you embark upon this long journey to stardom, find yourself a partner. Locate another person who, like yourself, is willing to spend a good part of her life for the next few years batting that silly volleyball off various and sundry bodily parts (including some places which you will never find discussed in any textbook on volleyball skills). By working with a partner, you can learn the full spectrum of skills and movements which are the tools of a volleyball player. If you happen to live in some

location where there is an over-abundance of volleyball nuts, you are in luck! Combination drills with three or more players will give you the opportunity to learn group skills.

Speaking of nuts, I would like to tell you that all of the volleyball skills which I have acquired over the years (since 1962), I have learned by trial and error, observation and hours and hours of repetition. Needless to say, I was never fortunate enough to have a coach to tell me to move my left knee this way, and my little finger that way— instead, I "made-up" all of my skills. I watched other players and tried to improve upon what they were doing. I would take the best parts of a skill from several different players and put them together for something closer to perfect. Nor have I ever been totally satisfied with my skills. Rather, I am constantly improvising and improving. As you visualize yourself as a player, you must realize that you are going to be a different type of player than anybody else ever has

SOMEHOW, FANATICISM IS so much more colorful.

been. You are unique. Therefore your skills will look a little bit different from anybody else's skills. Remember that it is your responsibility to form your own volleyball game and you can do this by finding the movements which are best for you. Keep in mind that your first priority is ball control. The quickest way to accomplish ball control is to move efficiently. This is no easy task—you must "feel" your body and respond to its needs and demands. You must be aware of exactly how it is behaving. You must never tolerate wasted movement! Did you know that most of the time people do not really know just how their bodies are

moving? When you get turned upside down in a Japanese roll, do you know just where your left elbow is? When you are spiking the ball, are your toes pointing or are they relaxed? These may not seem important, but by increasing awareness of your body, your ability to eliminate inefficiency and to learn new movements will increase by leaps and bounds.

In 1967 I was chosen as the Most Valuable Player at the USVBA National Tournament, was a member of the gold-medal team at the Pan American Games, and was chosen to the All-Hemisphere Team at those Games. I also worked out for twelve hours per day that year and could afford to eat nothing but peanut butter sandwiches. I am not telling you this story as an example of good nutrition, rather, I would like to point out that my personal development as a player was so consuming in my life at that point that even eating was secondary to me. Most great athletes experience a time period in which they seem compelled or driven to personally develop the physical and skill portions of their athletic selves. It is during this period that an athlete acquires skills which later will be the envy of the novice player. It is at that time when an athlete and her sport become one. From that point onward its skills will always be natural to her. It is an investment in time and intensity which can never be revoked.

READINESS

Readiness, then is the key to becoming skillful. When the need to master the game becomes etched upon your personality, nothing really can or will stop you. I am not suggesting that you will become a stark-raving-mad idiot like I did and start volleying everything round that comes into your hands (grapefruits, bowls, baby's bottoms, etc.), or sleep with volleyballs taped to your hands (in order to learn the proper setting position), or wear clothes made out of volleyball leather patchworked together, nor is it necessary to practice your dives and rolls on the dance floor on Saturday nights. It is possible to learn the game without becoming a fanatic! But somehow fanaticism is so much more colorful and dramatic and if you are inclined to the slightly looney side, go ahead and let it run its course! It won't last more than a few years, if you don't die sooner from the intensity of it.

Avoiding Diversions

I have outlined later in the book several key components to each skill which are correlated to success. If you keep these components on your mind and do not let your attention scatter to other minor diversions (such as what happened to that grapefruit at breakfast), you will reach a state of skillfulness much sooner. Keep in mind that you will never see a volleyball skill which is performed by another person that is perfect for you. You must test every movement for yourself. You must let your body "try-on" different movements until you can arrive at what is perfect for *you*.

THE ATHLETE AND her sport become one.

Practicing

In order to learn skills, you probably now understand, you will have to dedicate a good deal of time to finding and perfecting them. It is your responsibility to provide an environment for yourself in which to develop. You must find ample time and circumstance for practice. I have spent many hours in parks or on fields in the grass, in handball courts, on karate mats, as well as in gymnasiums, practicing. (I have even practiced volleyball in a few of those places!)

Mental Cues

I have tried to define the material so that you can concentrate on key parts to each movement. Try to give yourself mental cues that will help you to execute the timing, or remind yourself mentally of a particular part of a movement sequence that gives you trouble. I think that sports are essentially rhythm. When I play I am conscious of particular tempos of a skill. Sometimes I can change the rhythm of the movement in my mind and gain a desired change in my movement on the court. Experiment with this concept and see if it can't help you, too.

Master Original Material

Be sure that you feel comfortable with the basic components of a certain movement sequence before you go on to the next step. By building a good base you will form more solid skills. A solid skill will not let you down in stress situations. Always review what you have been learning early in practice, especially if what is reviewed is the basis for new material to be learned. If the review is unrelated to new material to be learned, try to learn something new before the review and always plan to try new things early in practice.

PERSONAL RESPONSIBILITY

By taking personal responsibility for selecting and teaching yourself skills, you will eventually have skills which are "tailor made" just for you. Constant preparation for each of your practice sessions will pay off in more meaningful practice time. If you teach yourself the skills of self-readiness, you will later become adept at preparing yourself to perform. This will make you a better competitor. In your practices, be sure you progress to certain stages in each session. You can concentrate your energies by specifying your goals. However, be sure you give yourself plenty of time and an environment to reach them. You will find that if you give yourself a proper base and enough absorption time and experience, you will be able to learn new materials progressively faster and faster.

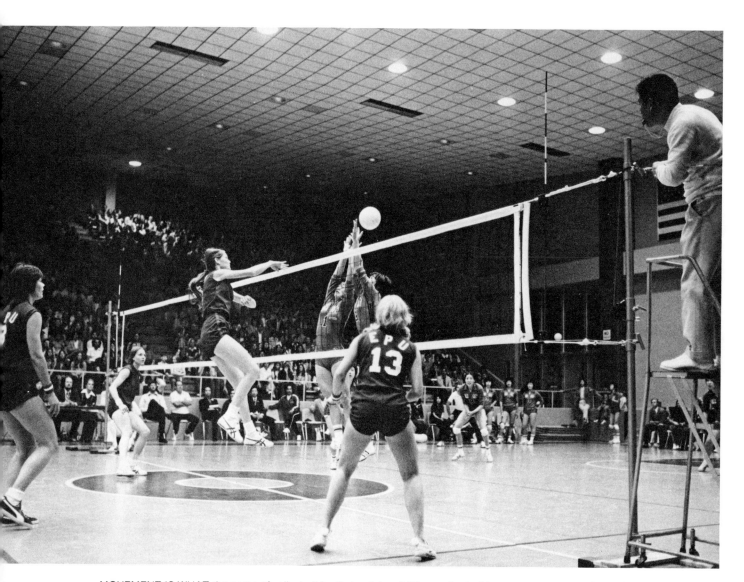

MOVEMENT IS WHAT the game of volleyball is all about. In addition, volleyball is a sport of grace and beauty.

chapter 5
MOVEMENT

Movement is what the game of volleyball is all about. If you combined the total amount of time that the players touched the ball in an entire match, it would total only seconds. What are the players doing all the rest of the time? Moving! Supportive movement or movement away from the ball is everything in volleyball. Further, movement is the primary communicator in the sport. When a player calls, "mine," there is still a good chance that she will *not* play the ball. But when a player moves into position to take a ball, she in effect has *screamed* to her teammates that she will play the ball. The chances are nearly 100 percent sure that she will then play the ball. Since every movement that a player makes on the court is, in effect, the primary way she talks to her teammates, it is imperative that every player on the court knows the language.

There are three types of communicative movement of which you should become very aware as you move with the sport of volleyball. First, let me say that all movement begins from a *ready position*. This ready position should consist of positioning your forearms at waist height or higher, palms facing with the elbows away from the body in a comfortable position. The feet should be spread comfortably with the weight on the inside of the feet and the knees pointing inward. This is a normal ready position from which you are expected to move and to transfer to other degrees of readiness. It is not necessary to play the game in a "low" position, the important thing is to be able to recognize when low position is called for and then to be able to transfer to that position quickly.

STRONG AND AGGRESSIVE MOVEMENT

All movements should be strong and aggressive. There is no place in volleyball for weak movement or half a movement. I think that it is a good idea to warm up extensively before even touching the volleyball. As you warm up, "tune in" to your body. Your warm-up should be rhythmical —almost to the hypnotic state. You should concentrate on your warm-up fully, do all exercises fully, thoroughly, systematically. This will prepare you mentally for the work-out. Always stretch after you have broken a sweat, and you should not start handling the ball until you are indeed sweating and a little fatigued from the warm-up. The fatigue of the warm-up should be only temporary, of course, from which you can recover in only a few minutes.

STARTING MOVEMENT

You should train yourself to always start for the ball even if it eventually turns out to be played by one of your teammates. A starting motion is very definite. It should tell all the players on the team that you fully intend to go to the ball. There should be no doubt.

STOPPING MOVEMENT

Once you start motion toward the ball, there are two things which you should follow. If the ball is your ball and you can make that determination, you should continue your motion toward the ball, gain body position on it, and make contact. You should usually attempt to stabilize as many of your body parts as possible when making contact with the ball. Further, you should always try to get to the contact position much earlier than the ball arrives there, the earlier you arrive at contact position, the more your chances of success are increased and the louder you are communicating with your teammates about your intentions. If, on the other hand, you have decided that it is not your ball to play, and have decided not to play it, you must make a definite and immediate "quitting" motion. If you cannot decide whether or not to play the ball, then both you and your nearest teammate are probably both making

weak movements and as a result are experiencing a lack of communication which leads to the confusion. In this instance you must try to make a verbal arrangement with your teammate regarding who in fact will play the ball. Call, "mine," or "yours," and make an exaggerated corresponding movement of continuing or quitting movement.

QUITTING MOVEMENT

A quitting movement is a movement which tells your teammates that you are definitely *not* going to take the ball. This movement must be just as strong as the starting movement, but you must be careful that you do not make a "distracting" movement instead. Quitting movements should be generally comforting to your teammates, therefore you must make this communication to your teammate early enough that she can proceed to the ball without hesitation. The most common circumstance for a quitting motion is when one player opens a "lane" to another. In this instance you will discontinue your movement toward the ball and turn to face the path of the ball's flight. I refer to this as "opening your shoulders to the ball." This serves a dual purpose: first, it tells your teammate that you are not playing the ball and second, it prepares you to make the succeeding contact on the ball. The second most common circumstance for a quitting motion is when you must "clear the ball." Sometimes two players are found occupying the space upon which the ball is descending. This makes that space a little crowded. Probably one of you has verbalized "mine" or "yours," but you are both in position to make the play. In this case, it is your responsibility to give the teammate making the play enough operating space to handle the ball. Continuing to occupy that same space is both intimidating and distracting, and it will almost invariably make your teammate unsuccessful. I have seen players

YOUR EYES SHOULD always be on the ball at its point of contact with any player. These Japanese players are intently focused upon their Russian opponents' hands as the Russians attempt to block.

who never touch the ball make teams unsuccessful because of this one common error. A player who continues to pursue the ball even after another player has gained contact position on the ball almost always make her team unsuccessful. Once it has been established which player is to make contact with the ball, it is the responsibility of all other players to make quitting motions and to clear the ball. Further, they must do everything possible to eliminate distraction through the point of contact.

EYES

Eye movements are a part of the movement experience which are given very little thought or attention, yet they are increasingly more important as your level of play improves. Your eyes should always be on the ball at its point of contact with any player. In between contacts, your eyes should be looking around the court. The information you will gather at these times will serve to either prepare you for your contact with the ball, or inform you of certain conditions on your side or your opponents' side of the court. In any event, it will always help to improve your personal perception of the court, players, and your specific relationship to the ball and the game. Once the ball has been contacted, it will not change the normal course of movement that the impact has given it. It is useless to continue to watch the ball when its direction will not alter. There are two exceptions to this statement. First, a knuckle ball, or a high speed ball should be watched. Second, you should try to watch the ball between the spiker and defender contacts. Being able to visually follow the ball after it has been spiked will have a tendency to slow the ball down in your mind, thus giving you better reaction time. If you are able to watch the ball after contact on the spiker's hand it also shows that you have overcome your fear of the speed of the ball.

You will achieve more comfort with any skill once you can take your eyes off of the ball. If you see only the ball during the play, you are experiencing a form of tunnel vision. Everything which is outside of the zone the ball occupies is therefore an unknown. Fear of the unknown can become a very real experience for you and your performance will be hindered because of it. You must force yourself to take your eyes off of the ball during points in its flight between contacts. However, remember to always watch the ball at the points of contact and at those times that I have mentioned above. Once you become comfortable with taking your eyes off of the ball at key times, try to access your teammates' degree of readiness, your intended target area, or the situation on the opposing side of the net by looking at those things while the ball is in flight. This is the final step in the movement experience toward mastering a skill and gaining complete comfort with it.

ZONES

There is an incredible crowding on the volleyball court when you consider six people jamming a space which is merely thirty feet square. And yet, sometimes it seems very lonesome with an incredibly large area to cover alone. The ball changes speeds rapidly in the game as does the concentration of action. Because of this, a player's court space responsibilities change. Volleyball is a sport of fluctuating zones. The zones change in size, in shape, and in location. There are basically two important concepts to grasp about the zones in volleyball: first, you must always try to balance the size of the zones and split them among the available players according to size of the available space and vulnerability of the available space. Second, you must have an arrangement with the players in the two zones bordering your zone regarding the *seam* of your zones. You must always be able to try for the ball without having any hesitation about a physical collision with a teammate. This split-second hesitation is usually the difference between a "dig" and a "kill" when you are playing defense. If you would merely make an arrangement with your zone partner about the direction of your effort, neither of you will be hesitant about trying for the ball. For instance, if you are middle back you could make an arrangement with the teammate on your right that would allow you to try for the ball in a zone which is behind your teammate. This way both of you can try for a ball which is hit into a seam between you without risking a head-on collision. In this type of arrangement, you would make contact with the ball at a lower or later point than your teammate would. In order to make this work, your teammate should not move backward to try for the seam and you should not move forward to try for the seam. Anytime that you experience hesitation because of a collision, it is your responsibility to make a pact with your teammate similar to the one which I have just suggested, which allows both of you freedom of movement for future similar situations. A word of warning here: it may take some time for you to actually be able to execute this concept, and specific practice of two players moving into a seam to dig a ball (but in different movement directions and from different zones) will be necessary.

(LEFT.) PRESENT YOUR striking surface to the ball early for best results.

(RIGHT.) EVEN THOUGH this player is completely extended in low position, she has stabilized her entire body over one leg prior to contact.

WHAT MOVEMENTS GIVE YOU BALL CONTROL?

There are certain keys to concentrate upon which will result in increased ball control. If you are having ball control problems with a certain skill, review these points in your practice.

1. Present the striking surface to the ball earlier. Especially in ball control problems where the faster pace of the ball is giving you trouble, get your contact surface presented to the ball long before you think it is actually necessary. It can never be too early.

2. Make all your contact movements in body line. For instance, do not reach to the side to pass the ball, get your body in a direct line with the ball.

3. Make all your contact movements toward the target. If you are following through with any part of your body in a direction other than the direction of the target, you are decreasing your chances of success.

4. Stabilize as many of your body parts as possible during contact. You must stop your movement and present an unmoving surface to the ball at contact. If an unmoving surface does not apply to the particular skill you are performing, you should be presenting a surface to the ball which is moving in the direction of the target area at contact.

5. You must demand exact accuracy of yourself at all times. Always practice with a target as your goal. Never just hit the ball up. If you practice with a target in mind, your skills will get better and better. Your practice time will be much more worthwhile and your skills will get better much faster if you will discipline yourself to always place the ball to a target.

HIT THE BALL at full extension.

chapter 6
SERVING

The serve can be an offensive weapon. But before you get too carried away making it a speeding bullet able to cut opponents' bodies in half, you must gain some skill. The toughest serve I have ever played against was the serve utilized by the Japanese women. This serve is a floater serve which jumps, dives, dips, and kicks to such an extreme that there were many times, when we first saw it used, that we were not able to even touch it, let alone pass it.

Passing skills are much improved compared to that 1962 disgrace and it is unusual now to be literally "served off the court." Gaining a good understanding of what you might do with the serve and then practicing to attain good skill will allow you to possess a serve which can be an offensive weapon.

BODY MECHANICS

Stand with your weight on your right leg if you are right-handed. (Left-handers reverse the instructions.) Place your left foot slightly forward. Prepare to toss the ball with your left hand. Raise your striking arm, keeping the elbow high and retracted so that the only motion necessary will be forward.

As you toss the ball with your left hand, drive step or jab step toward your target. Swing at the ball with a quick whip-like motion. The arm swing may come from the torso and thus be a front-back sort of movement or the swing may be emanated from a shoulder rotation, which I believe is more natural to Americans. So the movement sequence is: toss, step (weight transference), strike.

The ball will only go (1) in the direction of the swing in relation to (2) the point of contact on the ball. You should make contact on the ball with an open hand, gaining force from the heel of the palm. Contact should be made at the highest comfortable position in relationship to your body and in front of your body. The toss should be controlled and only as high as is necessary to hit the ball at full extension. The floater

PREPARE TO TOSS with your nonhitting hand.

TOSS AND JAB step.

serve is not for persons with pent-up energies. It is a very controlled, calculated skill. If you want to haul off and whack the ball as hard as you can, you will have to go to a high-risk, spin serve.

PRIORITIES

However, you might want to keep these priorities in mind: first, we want the serve to be in bounds. There is no opportunity to win a game if the serve is not in bounds. Accuracy is the second priority. You must be able to serve to a receiver or to an area anytime it is necessary. Third, you want to be able to serve a fast, tough ball in the court, with accuracy.

PRINCIPALS

Each service reception pattern has inherent weaknesses. Further, each team's weaknesses may be rated, thus identifying weaker passers and trouble areas. Each offensive system has preferred personnel and positioned receivers. For each rotation, a team will be able to receive a serve from one area better than from another. Certain players are "expendable" to the passing system because they have no offensive responsibilities. For example, the player who will hit the quick set in the middle is usually the last person a team would like to see pass the ball.

BEGIN TO SWING.

CONTACT WITH AN open hand.

GUIDELINES

There are certain times the serve must be in bounds and there are other times that a team can absorb a serving error and therefore a player may take a "chance" and serve a higher risk serve. Here are some guidelines for when you must serve in bounds:

1. The first serve of the game.
2. After a time out.
3. After winning a long rally.
4. After your opponents have scored two or more points in a row.
5. When a teammate before you in rotation made a serving error.
6. Almost any time that either team is within four points of winning the game.

Here are some guidelines for when you might take a chance of making a service error:

1. At the coach's discretion.
2. When the match-up of your serving errors to your passing ability is in your favor (especially in specific rotations).
3. When the score is within two points and neither team has scored half a game.
4. When trying to break out of the middle game and the score is not to your disadvantage.
5. When losing hopelessly and you feel like you can make it.
6. When you serve a string of points by serving with a progressively tougher serve.

THE ROUNDHOUSE SPIN serve is executed by applying a slice to the back of the ball on the upswing.

However, do not continue to serve tougher, and eventually force yourself to make an error. The advantage of series serving is to find a groove you can control.

Serving is your team's only chance to score points. You as an individual do not have the *right* to make the choice to make an error. An individual never has the right to choose to make an error, whereas a physical error can and will happen to anyone. Physical errors are excusable, whereas choosing to take a chance to error is a coaching decision. A chosen error is a decision to try to do something which extends the normal comfort zone of your skill. Each player has a different amount of skill and therefore a different comfort zone.

Your job as a server is to gain as much skill as possible and to be sensitive to the changing conditions of the game.

SPIN SERVE

Spin serves are easy to receive because their path of movement is predictable. The ball will only travel in the direction of the spin. The speed of the ball is what gives passers fits. Some spin serves can be very intimidating.

Spin serves differ from floating serves in that a spin serve is actually sliced. Unlike tennis, a volleyball slice is applied to the back of the ball on the upswing. The ball must be contacted behind the body in order to effect this type of slice. A spin serve is a high risk serve, takes more practice to perfect, and should be accompanied by some sort of barbaric utterance at the point of contact. A sound similar to a karate yell will do as an accessory to a spin serve.

THE ROUNDHOUSE SPIN SERVE

A spin serve may be hit from a normal spiking motion type of swing or from a roundhouse movement. The roundhouse movement is usually easier to learn. The roundhouse spin serve is executed with a straight arm slicing the back of the ball on

JAPANESE FLOATER SERVE.

the upswing. The ball is hit farther behind your body and contacting on the upswing slices and adds spin to the ball. A higher toss will give you more time to take a healthy swing at the ball when you are attemping to hit spin serves.

THE JAPANESE FLOATER SERVE

This serve is basically an underhand serve. Start by turning your side to the net, placing your weight on your back leg. Hold the ball with your non-hitting hand. Jab-step toward the net with your front foot. As you begin to transfer your weight, toss the ball. Each time you serve, rotate your arm in a higher and higher arch until you rotate into the ball in an arch above your shoulder. Attempt to make contact with the ball higher than your shoulder, not lower than your shoulder (as in the underhand serve). Ideally, the toss should be low, allowing for a contact with the ball at the top of your toss. By contacting the ball in front of your body, you will effect a more pronounced float. Swing your arm straight through the ball and allow your torso to follow the ball. Still more float is possible if you will whip your arm forward and increase the speed of your hand as you make contact with the ball.

CONCENTRATE ON KEEPING the platform straighter after contact than before. This will insure solid contact. Observe the lane opening made by this passer's teammates.

chapter 7
PASSING

Passing is the key to point prevention. If a team cannot prevent points, it may never get around to the other half of the game—point getting. Point getting will win the game for you, but point preventing will keep the other team from winning the game first.

BODY MECHANICS

Movement or body positioning is the primary ingredient possessed by successful passers. If all movement prior to contact is prepared properly and movement is followed-through toward the target area, good passing will follow. Passing movement should be fluid and deliberate. By moving your feet, usually in a shuffle motion, behind the ball and using a front-back stride motion, you may utilize a weight shift to aim the ball toward your intended target. When passing from the right side of the court, pass with your right foot forward. On the left side, your left foot forward is advisable. By thus "closing" your stance toward the center of the court, a missed contact on your contact surface (your arms) will result in a more minimal error than if your hips were open to the outside of the court. To further minimize error, you should pass the ball in direct midline with your body. Anytime you reach to the side of your body, you not only mess up the team's passing zones, but you take the chance of making a large error. In performing any skills, you should always take into consideration the amount of error which might result from a miscalculation. If, when passing, you move behind the ball, line it up directly in front of your body and then make motions, i.e. shift weight or arm motion, only in direct line with the target area, you will find very little that can go wrong.

If you successfully prepare these factors each time you pass, when you do make an error it will never be by more than a couple of feet. Anybody who passes any other way has settled for a sloppy skill.

BODY POSITIONING IS the primary ingredient possessed by successful passers. Use a front-back stride position. The ideal arm-to-body relationship at contact is a right angle.

YOUR PASSING CONTACT point should be a solid platform formed by your arms. Pass from a comfortable, relatively high-movement position.

CONTACT POINT

Your passing contact point should be on a solid platform formed by your arms placed well in front of your body. The ideal arm-to-body relationship is a right angle. This means that you must bend at the waist to change the angle of contact, since the arm-to-body relationship should remain constant. Passing should be performed from a relatively high movement position. Passing the ball one time one foot from the ground and another time three feet from the ground will only lead to inconsistency. A slight leg lift as you shift your weight forward should be comfortable. I prefer a drop motion with the arms after contact with the ball. Concentrating on keeping the platform straighter "after" contact than before will help insure a good surface through contact. Make contact with the ball in the middle of your forearms.

EYES

Following the ball with your eyes all the way to your arms will help you get constant contact. If you have trouble training your eyes to follow the ball all the way to your arms, try getting a visual picture of your arms "after" the ball has left. This will help give you a reference point to focus upon, thereby training your eyes to follow the ball better.

HAND POSITION

The most important thing about the position of your hands when making the forearm pass is to not think about them. It is difficult for beginners to make contact on their arms, so by focusing your attention on

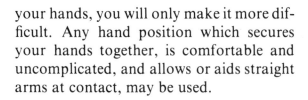

MAKE CONTACT WITH the ball in the middle of your forearms.

TRY TO GET a visual picture of your arms after the ball has left.

your hands, you will only make it more difficult. Any hand position which secures your hands together, is comfortable and uncomplicated, and allows or aids straight arms at contact, may be used.

COURT RELATIONSHIP

Your position on the court will determine what type of pass you will be required to make. For instance, assume that your desired passing target is to the right of center at the net. The cross-court serve is the easiest serve to receive because it is easiest to line up on. The cross-court serve requires a simple straight-ahead pass.

It is more difficult to pass the down-the-line serve. Body position on the ball is more difficult because you must move around the ball to "turn" the pass back toward the target area.

A STATIC, SIMPLE SKILL

Passing is one of the few "static" skills in the game. The area to which you should pass the ball is not usually changed from play to play. Most other skills demand that you make a choice of where to put the ball, dependent upon the particular conditions at any given time. So passing should be a simple skill. The ball travels at least thirty feet before you make contact, giving the passer plenty of time to move and react. As a result, passing becomes a concentration exercise. Once you understand the basic principles of lining the ball up and have acquired sufficient skills to physically perform, your determination and concentration will make you successful.

I PREFER A drop motion with the arms after contact with the ball.

BEING ABLE TO volley is part of developing "touch" in the sport of volleyball.

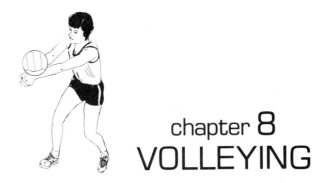

chapter 8
VOLLEYING

One of the most highly desired volleyball skills by beginners is the so-called soft set. Unfortunately, setting is one of the most difficult skills to learn because it is a timing skill and therefore takes many hours of practice to perfect. Being able to volley is part of developing "touch" in the sport of volleyball, much like one develops "touch" in basketball.

It is my opinion that the single weakest individual volleyball skill in the American game on all levels is setting. Setting is different from volleying in that setting denotes an ability to run an offense. Volleying refers to any overhand contact with the ball with the open hands. Setting is a specialization of the general category of volleying.

IMPROVING THE SKILL

There are several steps that must be taken before we can raise the level of volleying, and more specifically, setting in the United States. We must define the skill and standardize its physical components. Most important, we must provide a suitable environment in which the skill may develop. It is my suggestion that we change the policy, not the rules, of stopping play because of a mishandled volley.

The Japanese set a similar policy for the 1964 Olympic Games and virtually *eliminated* the volley on the first contact over the net. There is nothing to say that we cannot change our interpretation of the rules and make it a policy to *never* call an attempt to volley. There is much to be gained by such an interpretation, including extended rallies and a better environment in which the skill can develop.

DOUBLE PENALTY

Volleyball is one of the few sports which allows its officials to penalize a team twice for having poor skill. In most sports, a team or an individual is penalized for having poor skills or techniques by having poor ball control. In volleyball, we add insult to injury by further penalizing a team by stopping play and rewarding the advantage point or sideout to the opposite team.

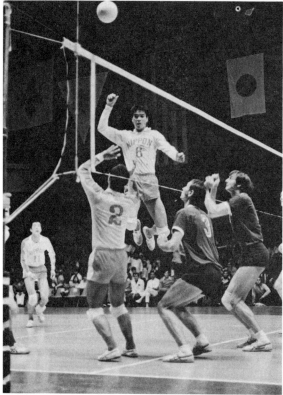

SETTING IS DIFFERENT from volleying in that setting implies an ability to run an offense.

If a basketball player shoots an unorthodox shot, the official does not blow her whistle and give the ball to the other team. In most sports, the coach is responsible for the technique that her players use. In volleyball, the official is the enforcer. As a result, officiating all over the United States is keying on different technique factors. Further, the inconsistency is impossible to deal with as a competitor. As a result, in most matches, the official is the central figure instead of the players. The game must be played by the players. I view the official's job as to, first, insure that a team does not take unfair advantage of its opponent and second, insure that the sport maintains its rebound format. When the official stops play because of a technique infraction at the expense of the rally, she is destroying the game.

THE OFFICIAL AS ENFORCER

Since the official is presently the enforcer, the development of the sport is hindered. It is the coach who works daily with the team,

IMPROVED SETTING WILL raise the level of overall play in the United States.

not the official. It is also the coach whom a player must please to become a starter. Once a player enters competition, she can become literally inept as an athlete by the disapproval of the official. In competition, I have frequently witnessed officials rejecting all the techniques that a coach enforces in practice. This problem probably occurs occasionally in other sports, but every time I witness a match in the United States at the college level or below (not to mention amateur competition), there is evidence of a power struggle. The leadership of our sport is in a constant limbo of authority. Specifically, volleying skills will only become better when coaches, rather than officials, assume the responsibility for technique enforcement.

CHANGE THE INTERPRETATION

My suggestion is to make a policy of not stopping play for a poorly executed volley. Five things will be accomplished by such an interpretation:

1. The environment for developing volleying skills will become positive.

2. The game will become more exciting for both players and spectators because of extended rallies.

3. The quality of the rallies will improve because of the increased ability to set the ball thus allowing for more offense.

4. The referee's job will become more consistent and enjoyable.

5. The level of overall play in the United States will have the opportunity to improve.

No advantage will be taken of either team by such an interpretation. Just as in all sports, the team which uses an inferior technique will automatically be at a disadvantage because they will have inferior ball control.

The ensuing information regarding the mechanics of developing the volley will help you to gain good skill. By coordinating these mechanics with a positive, encouraging environment for the skill, American volleyball will assume a new, improved character.

BODY MECHANICS

There are two primary factors which make the volley successful: (1) the contact surface and (2) timing. The first factor is by far the most important. If you do not form the contact surface properly you will *never* develop a decent touch. Once the surface is formed properly and contact is made on that surface, timing will develop with practice. Until this surface is being used, do not even attempt to make the touch "legal" or "soft." In fact, a little slap of the ball is natural at the beginning stages of learning to volley properly.

THE HAND POSITION consists of both hands opened wide, slightly facing each other, and placed above the forehead. Keep your thumbs behind the ball.

LET THE BALL drop into your hands, making contact with your fingers, thumbs, and the pads of your palm just below your fingers.

THE FLEXIBILITY OF your hands and fingers will "absorb" the ball.

THE CONTACT SURFACE

Ready Position

To form the contact surface, open both hands wide and place them on a wall. Be sure your fingers are pointing straight up and your thumbs are forming an inverted "V." Pull your hands off the wall, maintaining the same position, and raise them to a position above your forehead. Rotate your hands so that they face each other slightly. Now your hands are in ready position and properly prepared for contact.

Contact

Pick up a ball and put the ball into your hands so that you are making contact with all of your fingers (especially your first and second fingers), the pads of your palms just at the base of your fingers, and your thumbs. This is your contact surface.

Stand one arm's length from a wall with your feet in a front-back stride position and volley the ball to a place on the wall a few feet higher than the top of your head. Be careful to make contact with your hands in the ready position above your forehead. Do not "catch" the ball, volleyball is a rebound sport. A slight slapping motion is acceptable now. You will find that you must spend some time hitting the ball in this manner before you consistently hit *ex-*

actly the surface described and make contact with both hands evenly.

Once you are making consistent contact on the ball, you will be ready to begin to improve your timing. Be sure your contact surface is solid, however, before concentrating on timing. See if you can still get your hands to ready position and make proper contact when you have to move, for instance, or when the ball comes to you from farther than just an arm's length away. Be sure you are confident that you have the surface exactly right, because your touch will never become good with a lousy contact surface, regardless of how good your timing is.

TIMING

Place your hands in ready position and make one movement upward toward the ball with your hands. The flexibility of your hands and fingers will "absorb" the ball sufficiently. There is no need for you to make a deliberate movement downward with your hands or arms as you make contact. In fact, any downward motion with your hands or arms will only give you an inferior touch. Make contact with the ball as you move your hands upward giving a full extension to your arms and letting your hands move naturally forward at the wrist. Do not "pinch" the ball or flop your wrists all the way forward. As the ball leaves your hands, withdraw your hands back toward your head immediately. This withdrawal is the key timing factor. Try to make the withdrawal at the same moment that the ball leaves your hands. Be careful that you do not withdraw your hands backward or too low (below your forehead) and be careful not to jab at the ball by trying to withdraw your hands rapidly and ending up accelerating into the initial upward motion toward the ball instead. Accelerate faster and use more leg thrust only when you wish to gain distance with the volley.

THE EARLIER YOU get your hands up while the ball is dropping to you, the better your touch will be.

FOOTWORK

A slide movement under the ball landing with one foot in front of the other is the basic stopping motion for volleying. A slide is executed by taking one or more steps and stopping by gliding or hopping onto both feet which land simultaneously on the floor. A setter should usually set with her right foot forward but other players should volley with a closed stance toward their intended target area. A weight shift or step onto the forward foot is desirable at contact.

BACKSETTING IS THE same as frontsetting except for a forward hip movement, which changes the angle of your upward thrust, making the ball go backward.

THE BACKWARD VOLLEY

Volleying behind you is exactly the same as volleying to the front except for a hip shift through contact. By moving the hips forward at contact, the body-to-ball relationship is changed significantly enough to make the ball go backward. In the front volley, your body is behind the ball, whereas in the backward volley your body is under the ball. Your hands should begin in the same ready position and the contact surface remains unchanged for a backward volley. Your follow-through will be no different than for a front volley except the forward hip-movement will give you follow-through which goes behind the body, even though your arm-to-body relationship remains the same as if you were volleying forward. More leg bend and a wider stance will exaggerate the hip shift and give you the potential for more distance on the back-ward volley. A faster hip movement will also allow you to send the ball farther.

APPLICATION

You must practice volleying the ball until you have complete comfort with the skill. Jump volley, fall and volley, and backward volley are some of the variations with which you should work. Always try to volley the second hit in a rally. Any ball which comes over the net easily should also be fielded with a volley. I personally would prefer to see more volleying as a service reception technique. Volleying is one of the nicer movements in the game and the one skill for which the game was named. On many levels of play it has become a nearly extinct skill. *By learning a proficiency with the volley, you can contribute to its revival, which will improve your level of play.*

VOLLEYING IS ONE of the nicer movements in the game and the one skill for which the game was named.

UNTIL YOU HAVE developed two respectable power shots, you are functioning below your potential.

chapter 9
SPIKING

S piking is the end contact of the team's possession of the ball. It is the culmination of the team's effort each time the ball is returned over the net. It is the final extension of the total team's effort.

Therefore, hitting determines whether or not a team continues to participate in a rally. Further, it determines what options are available to the opponent. It is the vehicle for eliminating either team from the rally.

It is in light of these points that a spiker must regulate the choices of what shot she is to hit. The more a team's individuals extend their effort into the rally, the less a hitter has a right to make an error. Before we discuss how to make intelligent choices, let's look at the movement principles.

BODY MECHANICS

When spiking, only two factors determine where the ball will go. So, if you are missing your target area, you need only to adjust one or both of these factors.

Point of contact on the ball—if you desire the ball to go straight down you must hit the top of it.

Direction of the swing—if indeed you do hit the top of the ball, it will go straight down. If you swing sideways at the ball, it will not go straight down, but instead will go down at an angle.

To make the ball go straight down, then, you must do two things: (1) hit the very top of the ball, and (2) swing straight down at the ball. By remembering these two points, your corrections can certainly become simplified when you are not getting the results that you want. Of course, hitting the ball straight down is unrealistic since you must hit the ball over the net. Depending upon the height and depth of the ball as you make contact, choose the proper direction of swing and contact point to make the ball go to your intended target.

APPROACH

The amount of time that you are in the air

determines (1) the range of angles you may hit with power, especially with a flat hit, and (2) the amount of time you have to work with to move your body in the air. By improving on your jump, you will increase the amount of fun you can have as a hitter.

Most approaches are one- or two-step, pre-jump, jump, hit movements. The steps are similar to taking off from a diving board, with less upward exaggeration. Seldom are more than two steps necessary prior to the pre-jump. I prefer a hop movement before beginning your approach. This hop can be used as a readiness step, and in this case you would hop in place. If you use the hop as an adjustment step, you may hop laterally to line up on the set, then take your approach. The longer you can make your pre-jump and utilize the momentum properly, the higher you will be able to jump. The pre-jump prepares you to jump. It is a horizontal jump from one foot (your last step) onto two feet. From your pre-jump, rebound from two feet into the air to spike the ball. If your approach does not have a pre-jump, you will lose momentum and therefore not be able to jump as high. Once you begin your approach, make it fast, explosive, and fluid. You need to practice your approach jumps until they are automatic.

ARM SWING

I think that the most natural spiking arm swing for Americans is a shoulder rotation. This style is not always used in foreign countries, nor is it necessarily the best method for you. However, it is the motion which I generally recommend and therefore I will deal with it here. There are two common problems with this shoulder rotation arm swing which you should be aware of so that you do not develop bad habits.

1. There is a tendency to rotate into the hit with a low elbow, thus making a low contact on the ball.

2. There is a tendency to swing across

SWING BOTH ARMS high, rotate your shoulders, and cock your hitting arm before your feet have even left the floor.

the body and thereby only have the ability to hit one direction.

Be sure you rotate your shoulder into the hit, leading with a high elbow. If your elbow is kept high there is almost no way you can make a low contact.

As you jump, swing both arms up in front of you. As you bring your arms up, rotate your shoulders (don't leave your nonhitting arm behind) and cock your hitting arm. Keep your elbow high. As you start to hit the ball, rotate your shoulders into the ball, leading with your nonhitting arm. Shoulder, elbow, arm, and hand, respectively, rotate into the ball.

Review of Sequence
Approach.
Hop, Step, Step (optional), pre-jump, jump.
Arm-Swing: arms up, rotate shoulders, cock arm, swing.

USE YOUR NONHITTING arm to help rotate your shoulder back for a powerful hitting position.

YOUR NONHITTING ARM also drives your shoulder forward as you swing into the ball.

THIS BALL IS hit in the opposite direction of the original approach angle (*left*) by using a full shoulder rotation.

POWER SHOTS

Every hitter should have the ability to hit two power shots. On the on-hand side (when the set comes to you from the same side as your hitting arm), you should approach the angle shot. The angle is your first priority on the on-hand side. You should be able to hit that angle with good power. You must have the capability of hitting the ball inside the ten-foot line and well within the sideline. The mistake many hitters make in attempting to hit the angle is to let the ball drop too low. If you have properly set up this shot, you should make contact with the ball as high as you can reach and well out in front of your hitting shoulder. You must choose the contact point on the ball which gives you the best *down* angle on the ball, given the depth of the set and your leaping ability. Since you have already made an angle approach with

your body, once you have jumped you should make another turn in the air farther toward the angle which will give you several more feet of range.

Your second power shot is the line. Try to make all factors look the same when you hit the line shot as when you hit the angle. The first difference occurs when you make your turn in the air. Instead of turning farther toward the angle, let the ball travel past your hitting arm, make a turn toward the line and swing down the line. The most common error when hitting line is to turn past the line so your body is facing out of bounds. The result of this turn is usually an out hit. Be sure to stop your shoulders when they face your intended target and then swing directly toward that target.

By being able to hit both of these power shots, you should always have one of them available to you. By approaching the angle with your body before and after your jump,

YOU DO NOT have to be tall to be a spiker, just jump well. This 5'4" Korean player can compete with the best.

THIS JAPANESE PLAYER drives the ball into the blockers' arms below their hands to drive it down on the opponent's side of the court for a point.

you broadcast to your opponents that you intend to hit the best angle shot you can. If they do not adjust their blocking positions, hit it. If they adjust their block accordingly, you have "set them up" for a line hit. Occasionally blockers will be (1) poorly coordinated, (2) late on moving, or (3) stupid. In any or all of these cases, you may have a third power shot available to you: between the block. Any block that allows a hitter this power option is terrible.

When hitting the third power shot, approach the power angle exactly as you did when hitting the first two options. As you let the ball travel past your body as you did while hitting the line shot, just cut the ball off before it gets to your nonhitting shoulder and hit between the block. This same hit may be used against a solid tandem block that is reaching high. Sometimes you can let the ball drop and hit at the space between the net and their hands. In this situation, aim at the blocker's arms and try to drive the ball down between the blockers and the net on the opponent's side of the court.

OFF-SPEED

You should have a wide array of off-speed shots at your disposal to be a well-rounded hitter. Off-speed shots are low-risk hits and may be used once you have trained your opponents to respect your power shots.

DINKS

A dink is a soft shot which you control with your fingers or your whole hand. The one-hand-set type of dink utilizes a touch on the ball similar to the same touch you use when setting the ball. You should be able to set-dink (one- or two-handed) the ball short or long, starting from the same motion you use to hit. If the defense is utilizing a standard three-back defense, you should challenge the line digger's mobility and ability to read early in the match. If your opponent is sacrificing one of their players to dink coverage with a two-back formation, do not automatically rule out the dink options. You can dink successfully against a two-back defense by jamming zones and confusing responsibilities.

WHEN HITTING THE close set, increase your angle of approach to the net. Notice the high elbow to insure high contact.

NOTICE THE LATERAL rather than forward follow-through motion on this close set.

AGAIN, LATERAL FOLLOW-THROUGH on the close set prevents netting. This follow-through, unlike that above, follows a cut-back hit.

AN EXAMPLE OF a grind dink.

GRIND DINK

This dink is widely used internationally. The spiker pushes the ball into the blocker until she has made contact,then with a very quick movement *brushes* the ball out of bounds. The grind dink usually results in an advantage to the spiker.

TOP SPIN

The off-speed top spin dink is a hit which can still have some pace on it and therefore may reach its target faster than the set-type dink. The top spin dink is more difficult to read because the arm swing does not stop as abruptly before contact with the ball. This makes the defense respect the power hit longer. Top spin dinking is more effective

against the two-back defense than the set-type dink. Top spin is achieved by slicing the back half of the ball on the upswing.

OVER THE BLOCK

Many hits during a rally are not play sets. A play set is a set which the setter sets from the preferred setting area, utilizing specified hitting and setting patterns. When hitting a rally set, one which comes from an awkward location and/or has fooled no one, the hitter often does not have many kill options. As a first priority, rally sets should be kept in play. However, should a kill opportunity be available on a rally set, by all means take the opportunity.

The first option (or outlet) on a rally set should be a high, hard, deep hit, aimed directly at the seam between the blockers. This shot is difficult to field by your opponents defense, especially if the top of their block is unstable, and will most likely afford them a returning offensive option no better than a rally set. The key to hitting a successful top of the block hit is to insure that the ball crosses the net at a height comparable to the height of the blocker's hands.

Depending upon your range, you may hit over the block with more or less power without making contact with the block. By being aware of the defense which faces you, you will be able to kill the ball from rally sets utilizing an over the block hit if your physical abilities and/or skills allow.

OFF-THE-HANDS

The hit into the blockers hands and out of bounds is almost always a sure kill. It is easiest to hit off-the-hands given a close, fairly wide set.

Ideally, you (the hitter) will be positioned inside of the blockers. This position allows you to "wipe-off" of the blocker. If your spiking position is outside of the blockers, a ricochet-hit off of the block is necessary. This type of hit is risky because the blockers are given more of an opportunity to "turn" the ball back into the court. This is easier for the blockers since you will be hitting the ball toward them rather than away.

These are a few of the types of hits which

should be at your disposal. You must develop your skill first then begin to train yourself to recognize when the proper opportunities arise for you to use them.

EYES

Eye movement patterns are an essential part of the skill of spiking. In fact, without the ability to "see," you will not ever be able to utilize your skill.

Practice this eye movement sequence for good results. Look at:

1. The passer's contact.
2. Your opposing blocker(s).
3. Setter and the ball (through setter's contact).
4. The set direction.
5. Blocker and defense.
6. If there is time, (a) Blocker (as you begin to leave the ground), (b) A key defensive player.
7. The ball through your contact.

Jumping ability, agility in the air, and the ability to make the proper choices will make you a superior spiker and a valuable team asset. Keep in mind that until you have developed two respectable power shots, the defense will not have to play an honest pattern against you. Until you earn the defense's respect, you are functioning far below your potential.

BLOCK WITH YOUR hands wide open, keeping them strong and rigid at the wrist.

chapter 10
BLOCKING

As you begin to acquire better skills and play in better competition, blocking will become a necessity. Your success as a blocker will be determined by several factors.

1. Your physical abilities. The higher you can jump and the farther you can reach laterally and over the net, the more successful you can become.
2. Skill. Your movement on the ground and in the air determine your blocking skills.
3. Ability to read. Reading gives you the ability to narrow down the possibilities left to the hitter.
4. Timing and reaction.
5. Coordination of the blocker to other blockers.
6. Coordination of the blocker to digger.

BODY MECHANICS

The blocker should set her position directly parallel to the net at the best position in relationship to the hitter. Generally, blockers line up on the hitter's approach angle. A more extreme base position should be set in relationship to the approach angle on the deeper set than the closer set. Once she has established her base position, the blocker should watch only the hitter. Fortunately, the ball can only go where the hitter hits it. Therefore, by keying on the hitter's arm swing, the blocker can determine where the ball will go. The blocker should try to reach the ball as close to the hitter's hand as possible. If contact is made close to the hitter's hand, the angle of available court will be narrowed.

A squat jump without steps is recommended for blocking. Jump straight up and down. Floating blocks are impossible to play defense behind and limit your ability to reach in the air. Block with your hands wide open, keeping your hands strong and rigid at the wrist. Your contact area for blocking is similar to hitting. Use your whole hand, gaining force from the heel of

THE OUTSIDE BLOCKER shows excellent hand rotation on the ball to prevent it from going out of bounds.

the hand. Make contact on top of the ball in order to return it to the opponent's floor. Add impetus to the ball while blocking by moving your hands toward the ball. Initiate this movement from your elbow, block the ball on the opposite side of the net and return your hands immediately to a position over your head to eliminate hitting the net.

TANDEM MOVEMENT

When attempting a two-player block, the factors become more complicated because you now must coordinate your movements with a teammate. One player must assume the responsibility of setting the block, or determining where it will be placed. Usually the outside blocker assumes this responsibility. Once this is clear, the remaining player must become responsible for closing the block. The player setting the block must do so before the hitter jumps. If the outside player sets the block early enough, the middle blocker will be able to close sufficiently on the ground. This should be the beginning of a solid foundation to the defense. Assuming both players jump straight up (no travelling road shows please), the players must then recognize their responsibilities in the air. Each blocker must recognize whether or not the hitter is hitting at her. A hitter will have to hit in the direction of one blocker or the other or will hit the seam. The blocker whose direction is being hit should penetrate over the net and surround the ball in that direction. If this blocker cannot reach around the ball, and thereby eliminate that shot entirely, she should not "chase" the ball, but only reach straight over the net instead. This allows the defense to coordinate with the block. The blocker whose direction is not being hit is responsible for closing the seam in the air. When the blockers cannot determine in which direction the hitter is hitting, the blocker who lined up on the hitter's approach angle (on the ground) should reach the approach angle and the other blocker should reach the seam. Anytime a blocker reaches sideways, she must (1) penetrate farther over the net with the outside hand and turn the hand, (2) be sure she can reach all of the ball, and (3) be sure she does not open a seam which cannot be closed by her partner. Arm movements should be straight over the net or sideways and over the net. Blocking sideways down the net without reaching over is an ineffective blocking technique. Penetration is the key.

TIMING

Blockers must jump together and reach over the net at the same time in order to present a solid block. Try to start your jump for the block quite a bit later than the

THIS IS A good example of a well coordinated tandem block. One player is reaching the ball, the other the seam.

hitter's jump. The later you can jump, the more time you will have to "read" the hitter. Most blockers jump too early. Experiment with your timing by seeing how late you can jump. Ideally, you will be making contact as you block at the top of your jump, or on the way up. Blocking on the way down usually results in net errors and not enough time in the air at contact to control the ball with your hands. Getting your hands on the ball, rather than your arms, is easier when you are not descending, and affords much more ball control. Contact with your arms is always chancy.

The key to blocking success is determined by:

1. Setting the block.

2. Physical abilities of the blockers.

3. Recognition of responsibility of the blockers in the air.

4. The coordination of the blockers allowing them to jump together and reach over the net together.

5. The coordination of the blockers to the defense.

THE BEST BLOCKERS TO HIT AGAINST

The Hula-Hoop or Field-Goal Blocker

Unfortunately, no extra points are scored for shots which go between the uprights.

The Blind-Baby Blocker

To some, blocking a hitter is like going to a horror movie, they cannot bear to watch.

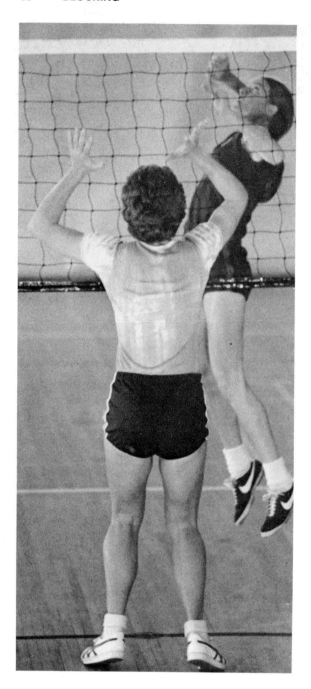

(LEFT.) BLOCKERS SHOULD jump later than hitters.

(RIGHT.) WHO SAID the blind cannot play volleyball?

The Indian-Giver Blocker

Show it to them and take it away. Hit anywhere, they are so busy being sneaky they will never make contact.

The Cheerleader Blocker

Leg splits could be disasterous to fellow blockers. Split blocks with the arms could be the cheapest way to get a nose job.

The Fly-By-Night Blocker

Also known as jump-on-by, teammates cannot trust these blockers to cut off anything.

Fly-United Blockers

A version of the fly-by-nighter. Ingredients: one player stationary, one player in flight. Voila—united!

SPLIT BLOCKS LIKE this could result in a rearrangement of features. Backcourt teammates could also have a surprise facial.

YOU CAN IMAGINE how excited a ball gets after it has been spiked.

chapter 11
WHY VOLLEYBALL PLAYERS DIVE AND ROLL

Volleyballs are basically empty headed creatures. No matter how hard you work to train them to perform, they will always hold a few surprises in store for you. I'm not saying that volleyballs are not trainable, they are just not "completely" trainable.

Your first training crisis will occur at competition. First of all, balls are social creatures and as soon as you separate a couple of them away from the rest of the group for the game, they get terribly excited and uncomfortable. Just the anticipation of competition will make the balls begin to frenzy.

When the ball gets excited, it is almost impossible to get it to concentrate. Many times you think you are really getting good at practice. You think that you have gained some ball control and are really getting good at the game. Then you play a match and everything falls apart. You are terrible, your team is terrible, and you wonder if you will ever win a game.

HYPNOTIZING THE BALL

What has actually happened is that you have neglected the most important skill of all: hypnotizing the ball. When you practice, the ball is completely relaxed. Chances are it spent the night with its comrades, or else you personally carried it all the way to practice. Since a volleyball is a social creature, this camaraderie with its kind, or personal attention from you, reassures it and puts it in a great mood for practice.

COMPETITION

When the ball gets into competition, many things change. As I mentioned earlier, the game balls are separated out from the rest. The excitement in the gym is very distracting to the ball. You are probably excited, your teammates and coaches are excited, and the opponents and spectators are beginning to anticipate the grand event. Each person who gets keyed up for this event emits an excitement zone in the gym. Every-

(TOP.) BY TRAINING the ball to associate a specific face or noise with a certain skill, it will become responsive.

(BOTTOM.) YOU MUST always make a noise at a ball that passes you.

body becomes more intense and animated at spiking points in the match—excitement zones reach a peak. Not to mention just the physical impact! Imagine how excited you would be if you had just been smashed out of the air and sent diving head first toward the floor at one hundred miles per hour! No wonder defense is such a difficult part of the game. Since the ball is in such a frenzy after it has been spiked, you must remain calm at all costs. If you emit an air of serenity around you, the ball will be attracted to your area.

ATTRACTING THE BALL

Just as the ball enters your zone, you can further attract the ball by (1) making faces at it and (2) making noises at it. Since the ball is basically empty-headed, you can never assume that it knows what you want it to do.

By training it to associate a specific face or noise with a certain skill, it will become responsive. Digging noises are particularly critical. Since the ball is so terribly excited, you must make a sound at the ball which is at a different tone from the excited noises in the gym, but at the same time somewhat reassuring and indicative of the type of movement you want from it. You must always make a noise at a ball which passes by

time a ball passes through one of the zones, it gets frazzled and bedazzled and it cannot concentrate; it cannot respond to you. There is nothing worse than playing with a nonresponsive ball—that one factor alone can turn a match into a nightmare.

Do not despair, however. Top players employ methods which quite effectively calm the ball down, get its attention, and attract it to them.

First of all you must be aware of the fact that the ball gets more excited at some points during the rally than at others. For instance, you can imagine how excited the ball gets after it has been spiked. Every-

you. This will show it how disappointed you are. The ball will think twice before passing you again. That moment's hesitation when the ball is considering whether or not to bounce could make the difference between digging it or not. Occasionally, you might make a total body posture which will tell the ball how disappointed you are when it eludes you, but this is not recommended on a regular basis. Balls get tired of playing with pouters. In fact, balls are generally very frolicsome. You must realize that no matter how hard you try, the ball will never be completely trainable. It's devilish and impish and will constantly pull tricks on you. Just when you think you have everything under control, it might jump up and hit you in the head, or take a nose dive between two players, drawing both toward it, elude both, and cause a collision. I'm sure if you have played at all, you have experienced several of the ball's little jokes during practice and competition.

FROLICKING

Actually, what the ball is trying to tell you when it eludes you is that it is in a frolicsome mood. When the ball is in a frolicsome mood, there is nothing you can do except join in and frolic with it.

When balls play, they are very alert. They are looking for someone to play with. If you won't cooperate, they will find someone else to play with, or they may continue to amuse themselves. Remember that every time a ball bounces, it looks back at the spot where it bounced. Every time it frolics past a player, it will look back before it bounces. That is why if you continue to try for the ball, even though it has already eluded one teammate, you may be able to dig it while its eyes are looking the other way.

RULES FOR FROLICKING (OR WHY VOLLEYBALL PLAYERS DIVE AND ROLL)

1. Always try for the ball with a volley-ball-related activity (frolicking) at any point that it passes you.

2. If a volleyball does not pass you, but bounces some distance away from you where you must move or run to intercept it, frolic as a follow-through movement (after you hit the ball), if it was a challenging chase.

3. In an unsuccessful chase, always frolic after the ball at the spot where it bounces no matter how late you get there. This will compliment the ball on its frolicking ability.

A volleyball-related activity is a dive, a roll, or a half roll. Knee slides and butt spins, etc. give the volleyball an identity crisis. Seeing these movements makes the ball wonder whether it has attended the right practice. Further, nonrelated volleyball movements identify *you* as something other than a volleyball player, causing the ball to lose interest in you since it is clannish and doesn't recognize other sports. In the ball's eyes, everything except volleyball players are inferior and therefore not worth its time. Remember that volleyballs are social creatures and don't like to do anything alone. When it makes contact with the floor, join it. There is nothing a ball hates worse than contacting the floor alone. Refusing to romp with the ball makes it sullen, obnoxious and most unresponsive. You must work daily to keep the ball responding to you if you expect any kind of training results. By creating the proper calm environment and frolicking by the rules, you will find you will be able to achieve satisfying results with even your old volleyballs. Once you have this type of success training the ball, you will have learned one of the most important skills in the game: "how to hypnotize the ball."

BODY MECHANICS

Your volleyball skills are not complete until you are able to make contact with the floor. Being comfortable with diving and rolling gives your body the freedom to fly around and have a good time with the game. By not having to worry about how your body might land, you can concentrate all your energies upon the pursuit of the ball, and proper frolicking, which keeps the ball interested.

Volleyball is primarily a rebound sport. Nonetheless, there are times when I do not particularly encourage the rebound format: when you are contacting the floor, bouncing is better for balls than for your body. However, I have found that bodies will bounce, not very high nor with much enthusiasm, but bounce they will.

PRELIMINARY POSITIONING

Whatever you do in preparation for contact with the floor, do begin the procedure from low position. Once you have dropped yourself to low position, glide to the floor. Diving and rolling should be smooth, fluid,

and most of all, painless. Hitting the floor can be fun. Having the ability to roll and dive and slide all over the gym not only keeps the floor clean, but gives you a grand sense of freedom about your body. There are great carry-over values too. For instance, you can dive just about anywhere. I know a volleyball player who is trying to set the world record for "most unlikely places dived in." World record categories could also be considered in these areas: most unexpected dive, most unorthodox dive, the dive disgusting most people, etc.

ROLLING

Rolling is simpler than diving. It requires the ability to sit down and perform a shoulder roll. To perform a roll to the right, take one lunge step to the right, go the low position, rotate one quarter turn to your left, and sit down. Lay back, rock up on to your shoulders and draw your left knee to your left shoulder. Use your hands to push

HERE IS ONE way to do a roll.

1

2

3

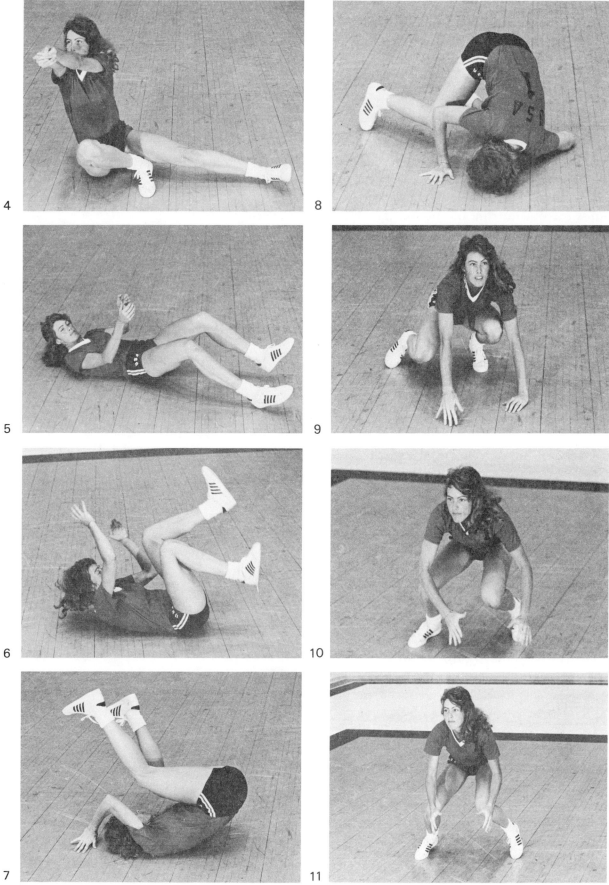

4

5

6

7

8

9

10

11

over onto your knees and your feet to stand up. So, all you have to do is step, go to low position, hit the ball, rotate on your foot, sit down, rock up on to your shoulders and roll over. Simple!

DIVING

Diving is more difficult than rolling because it is a timing skill. The beginning slide dive is just as simple as rolling. Take a lunge step forward to low position, place your hands far out in front of you on the floor, lower your chest and stomach to the floor, and as you contact the floor, push with your hands to effect a forward slide. This is a simple dive, the feet never leave the floor.

The advanced dive gives you more freedom and range of movement. It is a survival answer to high altitude flight. The advanced dive is exactly like the basic slide dive only one or both feet may leave the floor. Execute the same slide dive movements, but let your trail leg come off of the ground and kick up slightly. Later when you become more comfortable with this, let both feet come off the ground. Be sure to let your hands make first contact with the floor. By arching your back, the front of your body will present a curved surface to the floor which will absorb your contact and help balance your higher leg kick. Keys to success are assuming the low position, sliding as your body makes contact with the floor, arching your back, and keeping your head (chin) up.

Never dive until you are in complete control of your body. Always insist upon lowering yourself instead of by gravity, to the floor. This is easily achieved by taking an extra step to compose yourself after you make contact with the ball. By beginning with the basic dive and working toward higher (on your body) initial contact with the floor, and beginning to let your feet come off the floor, you will gradually develop a more versatile and advanced dive.

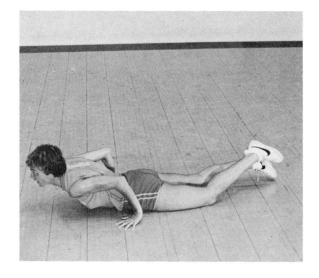

YOU CAN BEGIN to develop an advanced dive by beginning to kick one or both feet up off the ground as you slide to the floor.

This should develop naturally as you practice.

Every time you make contact with the floor, you should follow with an orthodox volleyball movement. This means a half roll, a roll, or a dive. Do not be responsible for some volleyball's identity crisis. In the ball's opinion, knee sliding is a second-class skill. If you do not mind having low-class skills, then keep sliding on your knees. If you are still sliding on your knees, then please stop attending volleyball practices —you are not a volleyball player. Believe me, the ball can identify the imposters.

DEFENSE IS EMOTIONAL.

chapter 12
DEFENSE

Defense is emotional. You must be prepared to crash and burn and disappear into a cloud of smoke, though I haven't witnessed many players actually depart this planet in this manner from a competition. However, there are countless rumors of such occurrences in dark, dingy, out-of-the-way gymnasiums. You must be willing to sacrifice your body with wild abandon, yet at the same time you must be able to assess the conditions of each circumstance. You must become finely tuned to the movements and capabilities of your teammates. You must know the game well enough to be able to read the play, because the ball travels faster than it is physically possible to react to it. Most of all you must want to try for the ball. You must enjoy physically trying for the ball. The defensive movement must be fun for you if you want to be successful. Mildly speaking, defense is the art of thrusting your body between the ball and the floor for various degrees of pummeling from above and below.

The defensive body (you) can be a projectile, a Hoover (the floor model), a percussion instrument, a hypnotist (be careful you don't put yourself in a trance), or a digger. The digger is the most preferable type of defensive body since the digger is the player who hits the ball up and into play. It is, of course possible to be a projectile digger, or a percussion digger, etc. and this is good variety for easily bored players.

Careful you don't become:

SLEEPERS—you may get rudely awakened.

SITTING DUCKS—at the mercy of the hitter (thanks to your blockers or the lack of them. (Also known as bite-the-bullet defense.)

A SPOILED BRAT—who would rather swear and throw temper tantrums than get the ball up. This player has some confusion with goal direction.

ACROBAT—the player who performs complimentary dives and rolls with no intention of ever getting the ball. Consult this player for half-time routines.

A COMBINATION OF sitting duck and percussion digging. Creative, but painful to watch.

Defense must be flexible. It must be capable of adjusting to stop what the opponent does best. The defense must be a reading defense. Reading is the ability to judge where the ball will go prior to the hit. The key word here is "prior." If you (as a defensive player), have not narrowed down the possibilities "prior" to contact, you may end up "reading" by braille, on your forehead. The only thing good I can think of to say about having Mikasa indelibly etched upon your flattened face is that it makes an unusual conversation piece.

BODY MECHANICS

Your lower body is critical to your success as a volleyball player because the movement of your legs is what drives you to the ball. You should start with a wide stance. It is easier to get to low position from a wide stance. Many times your success will be determined by how quickly you are able to transfer your body to the ground. Sometimes your body can "beat" the ball to the ground but many times you must drop

below the ball before it is even hit. If you like, you could practice drops and get-ups. I know one National Championship Team which practiced as many as fifty get-ups per day. At contact you should initiate some type of movement. Of course there are dozens of movements (at least) you could initiate as the ball is about to be attacked by your opponent. Unfortunately only a few movements that you "could" initiate are suitable for a lead-up to a defensive movement. Most highly recommended of the movements you might choose as you prepare to dig the ball is a "bounce" or "slide" movement to a wide stance. As you slide your feet farther apart, shift your weight forward. By moving your shoulders in front of your legs, you will insure some kind of ensuing movement, because by throwing yourself slightly off-balance, if you do not move your feet you will fall flat on your face. This results in an adaptation of the Mikasa face etching known as variation two: gym board sculpture. A ready position with your knees inward and weight

ONE METHOD OF cushioning a hard-hit ball is to rotate your hips forward at contact. This is most easily accomplished by sitting back after contact.

on the inside of your feet will increase your mobility. Always rotate your knees toward the intended target area at contact with the ball. This will insure better ball control. There are two common, and a thousand uncommon, ways of cushioning a hard-hit ball. I would like to deal here with the two common ways, your coach can try to deal with the uncommon ways.

First, you may rotate your hips under the ball. If you will maintain a stable relationship between your arms and your body (a

TRY TO MAINTAIN a stable shoulder base through contact. This is a fine example of getting the ball's attention by making a face at it.

right angle) at contact, but rotate your hips under the ball, your arms will, in effect, slice the ball, thus taking power off of it. This slicing of the ball can be effected by simply sitting down at contact.

Second, you may drop your arms straight back at contact with the ball. This cushions, or takes power off, the ball, too.

Try to maintain a stable shoulder base through the contact. I have found that by keeping your elbows away from your body (preferably forward, not sideways) your reactions will be better. Palms facing each other is an ideal ready position.

EYES

Once the ball has gone over the net and you have assumed your ready position, assess the potential hitters facing you. Then turn your attention to the setter and watch her closely as she sets the ball. Follow the ball until you determine set direction and the intended hitter. Once you have determined this and you have assumed your adjusted position, watch only the hitter until she hits the ball. As the hitter contacts the ball, fo-

cus completely on the ball. Physiologically, we do not actually see motion; rather we see a series of frames rolled together, as in a motion picture. Try to stop-frame the ball as many times as you can while it is moving. The more times you can stop-frame the ball before you make contact (especially in the last ten feet of its flight), the better you will dig. To force yourself to follow the ball all the way to your arms, try to get a visual image of your arms after the ball has left them. This will train your eyes to follow the ball closer to contact with your body until eventually the ball will *appear* to stop in the air, waiting for you to make contact with it. Then you will know you have truly hypnotized it.

Your most successful communication outlet is a strong, sure movement. Strong movements telegraph confidence to your teammates and let them know what your intentions are. Further, the only way you can get to most balls is with aggressive, relentless pursuit. Halting or stop-and-go moves almost never result in positive results.

READING. NOTICE THE hitter's alignment with the ball. Her entire body is behind the ball and contact is made way out on the hitting shoulder. Contact point on the ball gives you an indication of the exact downward angle the ball will travel.

Some of the keys you must learn to read are:

1. Relationship of the ball to the court. Example: If the ball is being hit from outside of the court, the line shot cannot be legally hit.

2. Relationship of the ball to the hitter. Example: If the hitter is making contact on the right side of her body and she is right-handed her best power shot will be angle on the on-hand side.

3. Relationship of the ball to the net. Example: If the ball is being contacted below the net or far back from the net, the ball will be hit deeper in the court unless power is taken off of it.

Your success as a defensive player will be determined by:

1. Your ability to contact the floor with ease and fluidity; initiating movement at contact toward the hitter; preliminary ready position (elbows away from the body, wide stance, weight on inside of feet, weight forward).

2. Your ability to read.

3. Your ability to hypnotize the ball.

VOLLEYBALL HAS BECOME a worldwide favorite as a participant and spectator sport.

chapter 13
THE AMERICAN GAME

As an American-originated sport in 1895, William P. Morgan developed volleyball in close proximity (both space and time) to the all-American game of basketball. Unlike basketball, volleyball remained a minor sport in the United States. Unlike basketball, volleyball remained undeveloped and unsophisticated. At least that is how the sport developed in the U.S. Once the U.S. Armed Services exposed the game to potential participants in other countries, it became a worldwide favorite. World championship games revealed that the U.S. was definitely not a member of the volleyball elite.

In 1964, Japan, not the U.S., introduced volleyball into Olympic competition. As the host country that year, Japan added volleyball as one of three trial Olympic sports. Volleyball enthusiasts around the world were thrilled. On a limited-entrant basis, the U.S. did not even qualify. However, because of a political mishap in Brazil (the 1964 Olympic qualifiers from our hem-

isphere), the U.S. was able to attend. Prior to 1976 the United States legitimately qualified for Olympic competition only once.

Probably the most dramatic influence on the game has come from the Japanese. Everyone has seen the brutal training film of the Japanese women's volleyball team. This is probably where the original crashing and burning into a cloud of smoke took place. There is probably no telling how many potential volleyball players were accidentally exterminated in this manner between 1956 and 1964. Undefeated for five years going into the 1964 Olympic competition, Japan captured the first women's gold medal. In this exhibition of kamikaze volleyball, the U.S. had its first exposure to what the world, and especially the Japanese, had done with our musty, measly, pat-a-pat sport. Intriguing! Wow! Have you seen those oriental women play volleyball? It was like a new dawning, a rebirth, an emergence.

In actuality, what had happened is that

PROBABLY THE MOST
dramatic influence on the game
has come from the Japanese.

the Japanese embarked upon a multi-year plan to win a gold medal. They knew they couldn't beat powerful, bigger, iron curtain teams using a power style. Matching power for power was not the kind of strategy that would result in Japanese victory. Thus, emerged the Japanese, and now the oriental, style.

Through much evaluation to determine how a team with smaller, quicker personnel could defeat a team with taller, more powerful individuals, Japan incorporated the now-familiar diving and rolling and the superfast offenses into their style. Also taken into consideration were psychological and sociological factors. Each girl was promised a husband after the Olympics. Each player was strongly appealed to in a nation-alistic sense. The six to eight hours of practice per day, 364 days per year, was for the good of Japan. Individual sacrifice was nothing compared to the glory of their country.

Being the Olympic host country, Japan was able to alter the game further to meet their needs. They changed the ball, making it faster, harder to handle. They made ball-handling interpretations which aided their style. Interpretations, by the way, that influence Americans today, more than a decade later. Basically, it could be said that the Japanese developed a style of the sport which was to their best advantage and imposed it upon the world. They were successful.

Since then, American volleyball fans

THE JAPANESE HAVE developed their own style in the sport. They are successful.

have been star-struck. Unfortunately, however, American enthusiasts have copied only the most dramatic aspects of Japanese volleyball. Needless to say, the fundamental reasons for Japanese success have remained unnoticed.

I think Americans should feel a responsibility to develop a style or type of adaptation of the game which will fit the characteristics and temperament of American athletes. Copying any other style of play will prove to force our athletes to underproduce because of unrelated identification and expression outlets. Further, our physical education background and the American athletic body type should be provided for in the style.

THE PROS

Recently, the United States assumed leadership in the sport by creating the pro game. The International Volleyball Association incorporated a totally new style of game by incorporating rule changes which drastically altered the game. The pro game places a premium on entertainment. For the first time since the American origina-

tion of the game, Americans are again innovators. For two years the International Volleyball Association (IVA) has struggled for exposure and expansion in their now southwestern-based league. The new pro game is both exciting and entertaining. As an outgrowth of this league, an American style of play is evolving. Hopefully, many areas will contribute to the development of American volleyball and the trend to mimic foreign styles will quietly die away.

THE UNIT CONCEPT

Regardless of what country plays volleyball, one requirement of the sport is its total reliance on team work. The very nature of the sport demands cooperation on the highest level.

The strict demands on teamwork make volleyball appealing to players and spectators alike. In fact, a well-functioning volleyball team is as near to cooperative perfection as any team can be. The team's success does not depend upon each individual's ability, but upon the amount each individual contributes to the team's performance. A team which has learned how to

AMERICANS SHOULD DEVELOP a style of play that fits Americans.

function (especially in crisis) has confidence and the knowledge to survive, even though the normal channels to success are blocked. The confidence built upon a team experience cannot be equalled. This is what makes the unit concept superior to the all-star concept. The team experience gives the unit the opportunity to acquire confidence in coaching, in fellow players, in their functioning as a team, as well as in the strategy outlined for them. A true team is composed of individuals who believe that the success of the team is of paramount importance. Each player transfers her ego satisfaction to the goal orientations of the team, rather than concentrating on her personal wishes

or individual recognition. Each player must understand and *accept* what her contribution is and will be. One outstanding attitude factor which must become an integral part of any team's psyche is that of total dedication to the success of the team. Role definition must always be of primary importance and each player must always know in what ways she is of worth to the team effort. This attitude puts a personal responsibility on each individual to train and become the most complete and accomplished player she can possibly be at certain points in time. It is her duty to train, to observe logical and intelligent training habits, or the success of the team will not be a reality. She must learn to gain satisfaction in a broader sense, from her personal contribution to a whole. The success of the team is further contingent upon the amount of responsibility each player accepts toward reaching the team goal. Each is responsible not only to train properly, but to be prepared mentally to make proper choices, and to make her teammates (each one of them) successful in her attempts to contribute to the team's over-all success.

You, as an individual player, must be prepared to totally believe in the unit concept and promote its ideals within the team framework. If you can't believe in it, then take up a more selfish sport immediately, before your volleyball turns into a pumpkin some dark, moonless night.

index